Let's G

MW01155944

Boat Rides

By Pamela Walker

Welcome
Books

Children's Press
A Division of Grolier Publishing
New York / London / Hong Kong / Sydney
Danbury, Connecticut

Photo Credits: Cover and all photos by Maura Boruchow

Contributing Editor: Mark Beyer
Book Design: MaryJane Wojciechowski

Visit Children's Press on the Internet at:
http://publishing.grolier.com

Library of Congress Cataloging-in-Publication Data

Walker, Pamela, 1958-
    Boat rides / by Pamela Walker.
      p. cm. — (Let's go!)
    Includes bibliographical references and index.
    Summary: Simple text and photographs present the experience of taking a ride on a boat.
    ISBN 0-516-23099-9 (lib. bdg.) — ISBN 0-516-23024-7 (pbk.)
    1. Boats and boating—Juvenile literature. 2. Boats and boating—Safety
measures—Juvenile literature. [1. Boats and boating.] I. Title. II. Let's go series.

 GV775.3 W35 2000
 797.1—dc21

                                                        00-025449

Contents

My name is Jane.

My dad has a **boat**.

We are going on a boat ride today.

Our boat sits at a **dock**.

It is tied up with rope.

I help to untie the boat.

The **knots** are tight.

9

My dad pushes the boat away from the dock.

Here we go!

11

On the boat, I wear a **life preserver**.

I wear a life preserver to be safe.

It will help me to float if I fall out of the boat.

13

Our boat goes fast.

I hold onto the seat.

The wind blows my hair.

Sometimes we stop the boat.

Sometimes we go fishing.

Sometimes I go swimming.

I don't swim far from the boat.

There is a **ladder** to get back in the boat.

My boat ride is done.

My dad ties up the boat.

Boat rides are fun.

New Words

boat (**boht**) a thing that floats on the water and carries people or things

dock (**dok**) a place where boats are tied up

knots (**nahtz**) rope ties that keep something from moving

ladder (**lad**-er) wood or metal stairs used to climb up and down

life preserver (**lyf** pre-**ze**r-ver) a vest that is worn to keep a person safe in the water

To Find Out More

Books
Boats
by Gallimard Jeunesse and Christian Broutin
Cartwheel Books

Boats Afloat
by Shelley Rotner
Orchard Books

Web Site
Boat Safe Kids
http://www.boatsafe.com/kids
This site answers many questions about boats and boating. It includes word puzzles and tips for boating safely.

Index

About the Author
Pamela Walker lives in Brooklyn, New York. She takes a train to work every day, but enjoys all forms of transportation.

Reading Consultants

Kris Flynn, Coordinator, Small School District Literacy, The San Diego County Office of Education

Shelly Forys, Certified Reading Recovery Specialist, W.J. Zahnow Elementary School, Waterloo, IL

Peggy McNamara, Professor, Bank Street College of Education, Reading and Literacy Program